W9-AZU-384

This book
belongs to:

_____

MESSAGE TO PARENTS

This book is perfect for parents and children to read aloud together. First read the story to your child. When you read the story a second time, run your finger under each line, stopping at each picture for your child to "read." Help your child to figure out the picture. If your child makes a mistake, be encouraging as you say the right word. Point out the pictures and words that are printed in the margin of each page. Soon your child will recognize the picture symbols and be "reading" aloud with you.

Copyright © 1992 Checkerboard Press, Inc., 30 Vesey Street, New York, New York 10007. All rights reserved.
READ ALONG WITH ME books are a registered trademark of Checkerboard Press, Inc., and are conceived by Deborah Shine.

ISBN: 1-56288-223-6 Library of Congress Catalog Card Number: 91-77735
Printed in the U.S.A. 0 9 8 7 6 5 4 3

Noah's Ark

A Read Along With Me® Book

Retold by **Laurence Schorsch**
Illustrated by **Pat Schories**

Checkerboard Press
New York

earth

people

Many years ago, so long ago that

giants still lived on the , God looked

down upon the and saw that it was

filled with wickedness. did not obey

the laws of God.

God became angry and he said,

"  are wicked, and I am sorry that I made them. I will destroy all the  that I made. And all the and  and creeping things that live on the ⊕ will be destroyed as well."

But there was **1** man, named , who was a good man. He obeyed all of God's laws.

animals

birds

one

Noah

Noah
people
earth
rain
forty
animals
birds

God loved and said to him, "Because the on are wicked, I will make it for **40** days and **40** nights. I will make a great flood that will destroy all the , all the and , and all the creeping things that live on the

. Everything that now lives on the  will perish.

"But because you, , are a good man and obey my laws, I will spare your life and that of your . I will spare your 3  and the  of your ."

And God said to , "You must build an  of wood and seal it inside with tar. It must have 3 stories and a  and a door on its side." God told  how big to make the .

Then God said, "You must bring 2 of each kind of living creature into the , 1 male and 1 female.

wife

3 three

sons

wives

ark

window

2 two

1 one

two

animals

birds

ark

 of all the, of all the, and of all the creeping things.

Male and female of each kind. And you

must bring into the food of all kinds

for you and all of the  to eat."

So 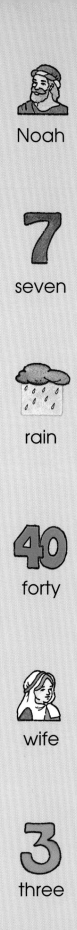 built the and did as God had told him. And God said to , "In **7** days it will begin to . It will for **40** days and **40** nights."

Then and his and his **3**

Noah

7 seven

rain

40 forty

wife

3 three

sons

wives

ark

Noah

two

earth

one

 and their went into the 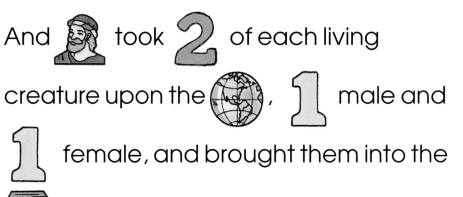 so that they would be safe from the flood.

And took **2** of each living creature upon the , **1** male and **1** female, and brought them into the , just as God had told him to do.

After **7** days it began to . And the  rose and covered the . The  fell for **40** days and **40** nights.

Soon all the houses were covered by ,

7 seven

rain

water

40 forty

earth

water

ark

Noah

and then the tallest trees, and finally the tallest mountains. And the entire was covered with and there was nothing to be seen except . And upon all the nothing could be seen except the . And all the living things on the perished. But and all the living creatures inside the were safe.

After the  had been covered with  for 150 days, the  began to go down. After **7** more months, the  came to rest on top of a mountain named Ararat. Now all that could be seen above the  was the tops of other mountains.

7
seven

forty

Noah

window

ark

water

earth

dove

40 days later opened the of the and let a raven fly out. The raven never returned. It flew back and forth over the until the was dry.

 also let a fly out the of the . But the returned that same night. reached out of the and gently took the in his hand. He brought her safely into the . knew that the could not find a place to build a  and that the 🌍 was still covered with 〰️.

👨 waited for **7** days. Again he opened the 🪟 of the 🚢, and again he let the 🕊️ fly out. This time when the 🕊️ came back she held an olive leaf in her mouth. So 👨 knew the 〰️ was going down.

nest

7

seven

Noah

dove

nest

ark

earth

After another **7** days, 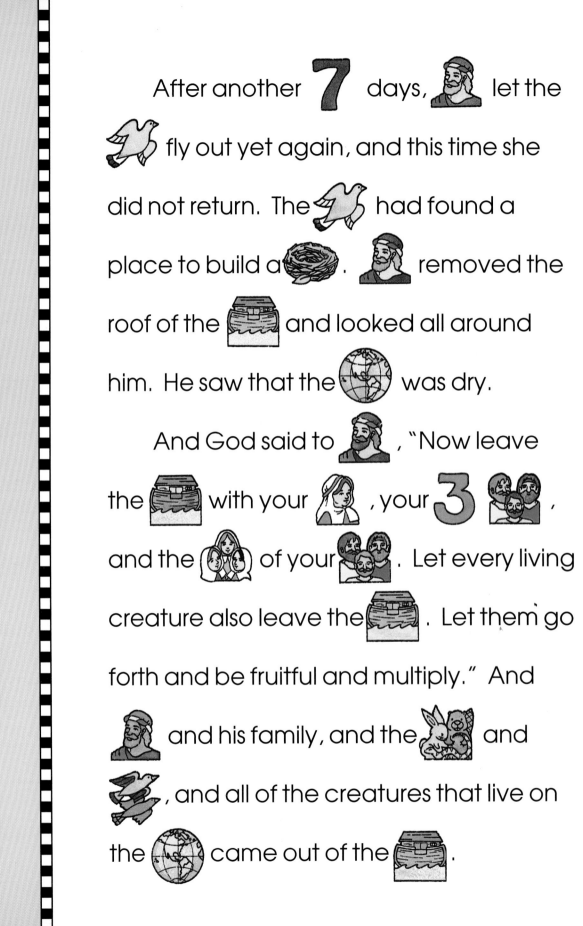 let the dove fly out yet again, and this time she did not return. The dove had found a place to build a nest. Noah removed the roof of the ark and looked all around him. He saw that the earth was dry.

And God said to Noah, "Now leave the ark with your wife, your **3** sons, and the wives of your sons. Let every living creature also leave the ark. Let them go forth and be fruitful and multiply." And Noah and his family, and the animals and birds, and all of the creatures that live on the earth came out of the ark.

wife

three

sons

wives

animals

birds

Noah

earth

rain

Then  gave thanks to God for saving him and his family. And God was pleased and said to , "Never again will I destroy every living thing upon the as I have now done." And God blessed  and his family and said, "To remind you of my promise, I will place a rainbow in the sky every time  falls. The rainbow will remind you that I have promised never to flood the again."

And  and his , their **3** and their, and all of their children spread out over the . And every living thing went forth and was fruitful and multiplied.

wife

3
three

sons

wives

Books I have read:

☐ David and Goliath

☐ Noah's Ark

☐ The Story of Jonah

☐ The Story of Joseph

The **Read Along With Me**® series is a collection of stories from the Bible, classic fairy tales and fables, and modern stories for parents and children to enjoy together.